DEVELOPING PSYCHOLOGICAL RESILIENCE

A GUIDE TO ACHIEVING BALANCE

DR. JAGADEESH PILLAI

|| Dedicated to all wisdom seekers around the World ||

ॐ

Contents

Contents

Prayer

Saraswati Namasthubhyam Varade Kamarupini
Vidyarambham Karishyami Siddhir Bavathume Sadha

Greetings to Devi Saraswati, the benevolent granter of blessings and fulfiller of desires. O Devi, as I embark on my studies, I humbly ask that you grant me the wisdom to comprehend correctly.

About the Author

Dr. Jagadeesh Pillai is a renowned Guinness World Record holder, writer, and researcher hailing from Varanasi, also known as the abode of Lord Shiva. With a Ph.D. in Vedic Science and a range of creative ideas and achievements, he is a true polymath. He is the author of more than 100 books including Research Publications. Although his roots can be traced back to Kerala, the people of Varanasi hold him in high regard and affectionately consider him one of their own.

In 1998, Dr. Pillai was offered a job at Banaras Hindu University, but he left the position after only two months to pursue greater goals in life. He believed that in order to study Indian scriptures and engage in other creative endeavours, he needed to retire from the daily grind of working solely for money at a young age.

He started an export business from scratch, using the knowledge he had gained from a previous job in the industry. His intelligence and unique approach to business led to great success in a short period of time, earning him more in just a decade and a half than he would have in a lifetime working in a government job. Upon the passing of Dr. APJ Abdul Kalam, Dr. Pillai decided to leave the business and dedicate himself to reading, studying, researching, and experimenting.

During his tenure in the export business, Dr. Pillai traveled to over 16 countries, gaining valuable insight and experiencing the world and life in detail.

Dr. Pillai has achieved four Guinness World Records in the following subjects:

"Script to Screen" - In this record, Dr. Pillai produced and directed an animation film within the shortest time possible, breaking the previous record set by Canadians. He has also received numerous national and international awards and recognitions for this achievement.

Longest Line of Postcards - For this record, Dr. Pillai created a line of 16,300 postcards on the occasion of the 163rd anniversary of Indian Postal Day. The event also included a questionnaire about the Indian flag.

Largest Poster Awareness Campaign - Dr. Pillai designed an awareness campaign on the subject of "Beti Bachao - Beti Padhao" (Save the Girl Child - Educate the Girl Child) to achieve this record.

Largest Envelope - In tribute to the Indian Prime Minister's "Make in India" initiative, Dr. Pillai created a 4000 square meter envelope using waste paper to achieve this record.

Attempted - 70000 Candles on a 210 kg Cake - To celebrate the 70th Indian Independence Day, Dr. Pillai attempted to light 70,000 candles on a 210 kg cake, which was recorded in World Records India.

Attempted - Documentary on Dhamek Stupa of Sarnath in 17 Languages - Dr. Pillai attempted to create a documentary on the Dhamek Stupa of Sarnath, dubbing it in 17 different languages. The result of this attempt is currently awaiting confirmation from the Guinness World Records.

Dr. Pillai is skilled in teaching the Bhagavad Gita, a Hindu scripture, and is popular among young people. He has helped many young people improve their lives through his motivational teachings.

In addition to teaching, he has composed and sung numerous Sanskrit Bhajans and patriotic songs.

He has also written and directed several short films and documentaries for awareness campaigns, and has volunteered with the police in both UP and Kerala to spread awareness about various issues through videos and photography.

Incredibly, he has produced and directed over 100 documentaries about the city of Varanasi, all on his own.

He has also helped and guided more than 25 boys and girls to achieve world records through creative and innovative methods. He is a multifaceted person who uses his intellect and the blessings given to him by God to excel in various areas. He is both a teacher and a student, always learning and teaching, and is able to master any subject he comes across.

He is a selfless social activist and motivational speaker who has overcome struggles and failures to become a successful and enthusiastic individual with a rich life experience.

In addition to his work with the Bhagavad Gita, he is also an efficient Tarot card reader, Astro-Vastu consultant, and a talented singer and composer. He has sung the entire Ram Charita Manas and Bhagavad Gita in his own compositions, and has sung the phrase "Lokah Samastha Sukhino Bhavantu" in 50 different languages. He is currently working on a detailed and scientific study of Vedas, Upanishads, Puranas, and the Bhagavad Gita. He has also composed and sung the Hanuman Chalisa and Gayatri Mantra in 108 and 1008 different compositions, respectively.

Awards - Four Times Guinness World Records, Winner of Mahatma Gandhi Vishwa Shanti Puraskar, Mahatma Gandhi Global Peace Ambassador, Kashi Ratna Award, Dr. APJ Abdul Kalam Motivational Person of the Year 2017, Mother Teresa Award, Indira Gandhi Priyadarshini Award, Bharat Vikas Ratna Award, Udyog Ratna Award, Vigyan Prasar Award, Poorvanchal Ratn Samman.

Preface

This book, Developing Psychological Resilience: A Guide to Achieving Balance, is a comprehensive guide to understanding and improving your Psychological Resilience. It provides readers with the tools and knowledge to identify and address the root causes of emotional distress, and to develop a healthier, more balanced lifestyle.

The book is divided into three sections. The first section focuses on understanding the basics of Psychological Resilience, including the importance of self-awareness, the impact of stress, and the role of positive thinking. The second section provides practical strategies for improving Psychological Resilience, such as developing healthy coping skills, setting realistic goals, and building strong relationships. The third section offers guidance on how to maintain Psychological Resilience over time, including tips for managing stress, cultivating resilience, and creating a supportive environment.

This book is an invaluable resource for anyone looking to improve their Psychological Resilience. It provides readers with the knowledge and skills to identify and address the root causes of emotional distress, and to develop a healthier, more balanced lifestyle. With its comprehensive approach, this book is an essential guide for anyone seeking to achieve Psychological Resilience.

I

Introduction to Psychological Resilience

Emotions are a natural part of the human experience and serve as a means of communication between our internal states and the external world. They allow us to experience joy, love, anger, fear, and sadness, among others. While emotions are essential for our well-being, some emotions can be difficult to manage and may interfere with our daily lives. These Psychological Resilience can have a negative impact on our emotional well-being, relationships, and overall quality of life. In this chapter, we will introduce the concept of Psychological Resilience, their causes, and the impact they can have on our lives.

Psychological Resilience Defined

Psychological Resilience are intense or prolonged emotions

that are challenging to manage or cope with. They are often associated with negative experiences such as loss, disappointment, failure, and trauma. Examples of Psychological Resilience include anxiety, depression, anger, guilt, shame, and sadness. These emotions can arise suddenly in response to a triggering event or they may linger over a prolonged period of time.

Causes of Psychological Resilience

Psychological Resilience can be triggered by a wide range of events or circumstances, including:

Life transitions: Major life changes, such as the loss of a loved one, a relationship break-up, or a job change, can evoke intense emotions.

Trauma: Traumatic events, such as abuse, neglect, or exposure to violence, can have long-lasting effects on emotional well-being.

Chronic stress: Prolonged exposure to stress can lead to the development of mental health conditions such as anxiety and depression.

Personality traits: Certain personality traits, such as perfectionism, low self-esteem, or a tendency to ruminate, can increase the likelihood of experiencing Psychological Resilience.

Genetics: The presence of a family history of mental health conditions can increase the risk of developing certain emotional difficulties.

Impact of Psychological Resilience

Psychological Resilience can have a significant impact on our emotional well-being and daily lives. They can cause us to feel overwhelmed, helpless, and disconnected from others. They can also lead to physical symptoms, such as headaches, fatigue, and stomach problems. In addition, Psychological Resilience can interfere with our ability to focus, make decisions, and engage in activities that bring us joy. Over time, the persistence of Psychological Resilience can lead to the development of mental health conditions, such as anxiety and depression.

In conclusion, Psychological Resilience are an inevitable part of life and can have a significant impact on our emotional well-being and daily lives. Understanding the causes and impact of Psychological Resilience is the first step in developing strategies for managing them effectively. In the next chapters, we will delve deeper into the specific strategies for achieving emotional well-being in the face of Psychological Resilience.

"The key to Psychological Resilience is to
focus on the present moment and be mindful
of your thoughts and feelings."

ജ

II

Deconstructing Psychological Resilience

Emotions can be complex and difficult to understand, especially when they are intense or prolonged. However, understanding the underlying components of Psychological Resilience can help us to better manage them and achieve emotional well-being. In this chapter, we will explore the different elements of Psychological Resilience and how they can impact our lives.

Emotional Intensity

Emotional intensity refers to the strength or weakness of an emotion. Psychological Resilience are often characterized by their intensity, which can make them overwhelming and difficult to manage. For example, feelings of anxiety may be so intense that they interfere with daily activities, such as sleeping, eating, or working. Similarly, feelings of sadness may be so overwhelming that they lead to a loss of motivation and engagement in activities.

Emotional Duration

Emotional duration refers to the length of time an emotion lasts. Psychological Resilience are often prolonged and persistent, lasting for weeks, months, or even years. This persistent nature of Psychological Resilience can make them challenging to manage and can have a negative impact on emotional well-being. For example, feelings of depression may last for months, causing a persistent sense of sadness, hopelessness, and fatigue.

Emotional Intensity vs. Emotional Duration

The intensity and duration of an emotion can interact in complex ways, affecting our experience and management of Psychological Resilience. For example, a short-lived but intense emotion, such as anger, may cause immediate distress but may also dissipate quickly. On the other hand, a prolonged but low-intensity emotion, such as mild sadness, may persist for a long time but may be less overwhelming. Understanding the interplay between emotional intensity and duration can help us to better manage and cope with Psychological Resilience.

Emotional Triggers

Emotional triggers are events or circumstances that evoke an emotional response. Psychological Resilience are often triggered by stressful or traumatic experiences, such as the loss of a loved one, relationship difficulties, or exposure to violence. Understanding the specific triggers of Psychological Resilience can help us to anticipate and prepare for them, reducing their impact on our lives.

Emotional Reactions

Emotional reactions refer to the behavioral and physiological responses that occur in response to an emotion. Psychological Resilience can elicit a range of emotional reactions, such as avoidance, irritability, or physical symptoms. Understanding our emotional reactions to Psychological Resilience can help us to better manage them and reduce their impact on our lives.

In conclusion, Psychological Resilience are complex and can be difficult to understand and manage. By deconstructing Psychological Resilience into their underlying components, such as emotional intensity, duration, triggers, and reactions, we can gain a deeper understanding of our emotional experiences and develop effective strategies for achieving emotional well-being. In the next chapters, we will delve deeper into the specific strategies for managing and coping with Psychological Resilience.

"Self-care is essential for Psychological Resilience; take time to nurture yourself and your relationships."

ଚଓ

III

Identifying the Sources of Psychological Resilience

Psychological Resilience can be triggered by a variety of internal and external sources, ranging from personal experiences to larger societal issues. Understanding the sources of Psychological Resilience is an important step in achieving emotional well-being and developing effective coping strategies. In this chapter, we will explore the different sources of Psychological Resilience and how they can impact our lives.

Internal Sources of Psychological Resilience

Internal sources of Psychological Resilience are related to personal experiences, thoughts, and beliefs. These sources can include:

Childhood experiences: Childhood experiences, such as abuse, neglect, or trauma, can have a lasting impact on our emotional well-being and can contribute to the development of Psychological Resilience, such as anxiety or depression.

Personal beliefs and values: Personal beliefs and values, such as self-esteem, can influence our emotional experiences and contribute to the development of Psychological Resilience, such as shame or guilt.

Thoughts and attitudes: Negative thoughts and attitudes, such as self-criticism or perfectionism, can contribute to the development of Psychological Resilience, such as anxiety or depression.

Internal sources of Psychological Resilience can be challenging to address, as they are deeply ingrained and often unconscious. However, by exploring and addressing these sources, individuals can develop a deeper understanding of their emotional experiences and develop effective strategies for achieving emotional well-being.

External Sources of Psychological Resilience

External sources of Psychological Resilience are related to environmental factors and external events. These sources can include:

Life events: Life events, such as loss, trauma, or conflict, can trigger Psychological Resilience and have a lasting impact on our emotional well-being.

Societal issues: Societal issues, such as discrimination or inequality, can contribute to the development of Psychological Resilience, such as anger or frustration.

Work-related stress: Work-related stress, such as job insecurity or high workload, can contribute to the development of Psychological Resilience, such as anxiety or depression.

External sources of Psychological Resilience can be more easily identified and addressed, as they are related to specific events or circumstances. However, they may also require a broader perspective and societal changes to address effectively.

The Interplay between Internal and External Sources

The sources of Psychological Resilience are not always distinct, and they can interact in complex ways. For example, childhood experiences can influence personal beliefs and attitudes, which can in turn contribute to the development of Psychological Resilience in response to external events. Similarly, societal issues can contribute to work-related stress, which can trigger Psychological Resilience related to personal beliefs and values.

In conclusion, Psychological Resilience can be triggered by a variety of internal and external sources. Understanding the sources of Psychological Resilience is an important step in achieving emotional well-being and developing effective coping strategies. By exploring and addressing these sources, individuals can gain a deeper understanding of their emotional experiences and develop a more comprehensive approach to managing Psychological Resilience. In the next chapters, we will delve deeper into the specific strategies for managing and coping with Psychological Resilience.

"The journey to Psychological Resilience begins with self-awareness and understanding."

☙

IV
Developing Awareness of Psychological Resilience

Developing awareness of Psychological Resilience is an essential step in achieving emotional well-being and developing effective coping strategies. When we become aware of our emotions, we can understand why we are feeling a certain way, and we can take steps to manage and cope with these emotions. In this chapter, we will explore the importance of developing emotional awareness and the strategies for doing so.

Why Develop Emotional Awareness

Developing emotional awareness allows us to better understand and manage our emotions, which in turn can lead to improved mental health and well-being. When we are aware of our emotions, we can:

Identify the sources of our emotions: By becoming aware of our emotions, we can identify the sources of our emotions and understand why we are feeling a certain way. This can help us to develop effective coping strategies and to address the underlying issues contributing to our emotions.

Improve our self-awareness: Developing emotional awareness can also improve our self-awareness, which can help us to understand our strengths and weaknesses, and to identify patterns in our behavior.

Enhance our relationships: Being aware of our emotions can also help us to better understand the emotions of others and to enhance our relationships with others.

Reduce stress and anxiety: Developing emotional awareness can also help to reduce stress and anxiety, as we can identify and manage our emotions more effectively.

Strategies for Developing Emotional Awareness

There are several strategies for developing emotional awareness, including:

Mindfulness: Mindfulness is a practice that involves focusing on the present moment and paying attention to our thoughts and emotions. Mindfulness can help us to become more aware of our emotions and to manage them more effectively.

Journaling: Journaling is a great way to reflect on our emotions and to gain insight into our thoughts and feelings. Writing about our experiences can help us to identify patterns and to develop a better understanding of our emotions.

Therapy: Therapy can be a helpful tool for developing emotional awareness. A therapist can help us to understand our emotions, to identify the sources of our emotions, and to develop effective coping strategies.

Meditation: Meditation is a practice that involves focusing on the present moment and reducing distractions. Meditation can help us to become more aware of our thoughts and emotions and to manage them more effectively.

Body-based practices: Body-based practices, such as yoga or tai chi, can help us to become more aware of our emotions and to manage them more effectively. These practices involve connecting with our bodies and paying attention to our sensations and emotions.

In conclusion, developing emotional awareness is an essential step in achieving emotional well-being and developing effective coping strategies. By becoming aware of our emotions, we can identify the sources of our emotions, understand why we are feeling a certain way, and develop effective strategies for managing our emotions. In the next chapters, we will delve deeper into the specific strategies for managing and coping with Psychological Resilience.

"The power of positive thinking can help you
create a more balanced emotional state."

☙

V

Understanding the Nature of Psychological Resilience

Psychological Resilience are a normal part of the human experience. They are often challenging to deal with, but it is essential to understand their nature to be able to manage them effectively. In this chapter, we will explore the nature of Psychological Resilience and how they can impact our mental and emotional well-being.

What are Psychological Resilience?

Psychological Resilience are intense and uncomfortable feelings that are often associated with negative experiences or situations. Examples of Psychological Resilience include anger, fear, sadness, guilt, and shame. These emotions can be triggered by a variety of factors, such as personal events, relationships, work, health, and finances.

The Impact of Psychological Resilience on Mental and Emotional Well-Being

Psychological Resilience can have a significant impact on our mental and emotional well-being. When we experience Psychological Resilience, it can be challenging to manage them effectively, which can lead to negative consequences, such as stress, anxiety, depression, and substance abuse.

In addition, Psychological Resilience can impact our relationships and quality of life. For example, anger can cause conflicts and strain relationships, while fear and anxiety can limit our ability to enjoy life and experience new things.

The Role of Psychological Resilience in Emotional Regulation

Psychological Resilience can play a vital role in our emotional regulation and self-awareness. When we experience Psychological Resilience, it can help us to identify what is important to us, and to develop our emotional intelligence.

For example, experiencing anger can help us to understand our boundaries and to protect ourselves from harm. Sadness can help us to understand our grief and to process our losses. Fear and anxiety can help us to identify potential threats and to protect ourselves.

Managing Psychological Resilience

Managing Psychological Resilience is an essential step in achieving emotional well-being. By understanding the nature of Psychological Resilience, we can develop effective strategies for managing and coping with them.

In the following chapters, we will explore specific strategies for managing and coping with Psychological Resilience, including mindfulness, therapy, journaling, and body-based practices. We will also examine the role of self-care and self-compassion in managing Psychological Resilience and achieving emotional well-being.

In conclusion, understanding the nature of Psychological Resilience is an important step in achieving emotional well-being. By developing an understanding of the role of Psychological Resilience in emotional regulation and self-awareness, we can develop effective strategies for managing and coping with these emotions. By doing so, we can improve our mental and emotional well-being and enhance our quality of life.

"It's important to recognize and accept your emotions, both positive and negative, in order to achieve Psychological Resilience."

ॐ

VI
Practicing Acceptance of Psychological Resilience

Acceptance is a crucial component in managing Psychological Resilience and achieving emotional well-being. Acceptance means acknowledging the presence of Psychological Resilience and allowing ourselves to experience them without judgment or resistance. It is a powerful tool for managing Psychological Resilience and improving our mental and emotional well-being.

Why is Acceptance Important?

Acceptance is important because it allows us to experience Psychological Resilience without trying to control or avoid them. When we resist or avoid Psychological Resilience, we prolong their impact and increase our distress. However, when we practice acceptance, we reduce our suffering and increase our ability to manage these emotions effectively.

In addition, acceptance can help us to develop self-awareness and improve our emotional regulation. When we accept Psychological Resilience, we can become more aware of our thoughts, feelings, and behaviors, and learn how to respond in a healthy and adaptive way.

How to Practice Acceptance of Psychological Resilience

Practicing acceptance of Psychological Resilience requires patience, commitment, and a willingness to explore our emotions without judgment. Here are some practical steps for practicing acceptance of Psychological Resilience:

Acknowledge the presence of Psychological Resilience:

The first step in practicing acceptance is to acknowledge the presence of Psychological Resilience. This means recognizing that Psychological Resilience are a normal part of the human experience and that it is okay to feel them.

Allow yourself to experience Psychological Resilience:

Once you have acknowledged the presence of Psychological Resilience, allow yourself to experience them without trying to control or avoid them. This means allowing yourself to feel the emotions without judgment or resistance.

Practice mindfulness:

Mindfulness is a powerful tool for practicing acceptance. By focusing on the present moment and accepting your emotions as they are, you can reduce stress and increase your ability to manage Psychological Resilience.

Engage in body-based practices:

Body-based practices, such as yoga, tai chi, or deep breathing, can help you to practice acceptance by connecting you with your emotions and reducing stress.

Cultivate self-compassion:

Self-compassion is an essential component of acceptance. By treating yourself with kindness and understanding, you can reduce your suffering and increase your ability to manage Psychological Resilience.

Seek professional help:

If you are struggling with Psychological Resilience, it may be helpful to seek professional help, such as therapy or counseling. A therapist can provide you with additional tools and support for managing Psychological Resilience.

In conclusion, practicing acceptance of Psychological Resilience is a critical step in managing Psychological Resilience and achieving emotional well-being. By acknowledging the presence of Psychological Resilience and allowing ourselves to experience them without judgment or resistance, we can reduce our suffering and increase our ability to manage these emotions effectively.

With patience, commitment, and a willingness to explore our emotions, we can develop a healthier relationship with our emotions and improve our mental and emotional well-being.

"The best way to cultivate Psychological Resilience is to practice self-compassion and kindness."

&

VII

Understanding Cognitive Distortions and How to Reframe Them

Cognitive distortions are negative patterns of thought that can contribute to Psychological Resilience and emotional distress. They are automatic and unconscious thought patterns that can cause us to perceive the world in a negative or irrational way. Understanding cognitive distortions and learning how to reframe them is an important aspect of managing Psychological Resilience and achieving emotional well-being.

Types of Cognitive Distortions

There are many different types of cognitive distortions, but some of the most common ones include:

All-or-nothing thinking: This is the tendency to see things in black and white, either/or terms, without considering the nuances or complexities of a situation.

Overgeneralization: This is the tendency to make broad conclusions based on limited experiences or evidence.

Mental Filter: This is the tendency to focus exclusively on negative experiences, while ignoring or downplaying positive experiences.

Disqualifying the Positive: This is the tendency to reject positive experiences or evidence because they don't fit our negative belief system.

Mind Reading: This is the tendency to assume that we know what others are thinking or feeling, without checking with them.

Fortune Telling: This is the tendency to predict the future in a negative or pessimistic way, without considering alternative outcomes.

Magnification or Minimization: This is the tendency to exaggerate the importance of negative experiences and downplay the importance of positive experiences.

How to Reframe Cognitive Distortions

Reframing cognitive distortions involves recognizing and challenging these negative patterns of thought and replacing them with more positive and accurate ways of thinking. Here are some practical steps for reframing cognitive distortions:

Become aware of your thoughts: The first step in reframing cognitive distortions is to become aware of your thoughts. Pay attention to your thoughts and take note of any negative or irrational patterns.

Challenge negative thoughts: Once you have identified negative patterns of thought, challenge them by asking yourself if they are based on facts or if they are simply assumptions.

Replace negative thoughts with positive ones: After challenging negative thoughts, replace them with more positive and accurate ways of thinking. For example, instead of thinking "I always fail," try reframing this thought as "I may have failed this time, but I have also had successes in the past, and I can learn from my failures to succeed in the future."

Practice mindfulness: Mindfulness can help you to become more aware of your thoughts and to challenge negative patterns of thought. By focusing on the present moment and accepting your thoughts and emotions as they are, you can increase your ability to reframe negative thoughts.

Seek professional help: If you struggle with negative patterns of thought, it may be helpful to seek professional help, such as therapy or counseling. A therapist can help you to identify and reframe negative thoughts and improve your emotional well-being.

In conclusion, understanding cognitive distortions and learning how to reframe them is an important aspect of managing Psychological Resilience and achieving emotional well-being. By recognizing and challenging negative patterns of thought and replacing them with positive and accurate ways of thinking, we can improve our emotional regulation and reduce our suffering. With practice, we can develop a healthier relationship with our thoughts and emotions and achieve greater emotional well-being.

"Take time to reflect on your emotions and
how they affect your life and relationships."

෪

VIII
Developing Self-Compassion

Self-compassion is a critical aspect of emotional well-being and is essential for dealing with Psychological Resilience. Self-compassion refers to the ability to treat oneself with kindness, care, and understanding in the face of difficult experiences, such as emotions, failures, and setbacks. It involves recognizing and accepting one's own flaws and limitations, rather than judging or criticizing oneself harshly.

Benefits of Self-Compassion

Research has shown that self-compassion is associated with several positive outcomes, including:

Reduced anxiety and depression: Self-compassion has been found to be effective in reducing symptoms of anxiety and depression.

Improved emotional regulation: Self-compassion helps individuals to regulate their emotions more effectively, especially in the face of difficult experiences.

Enhanced resilience: Self-compassion can increase resilience and help individuals to bounce back from setbacks and failures.

Increased happiness: Self-compassion has been linked to greater happiness and life satisfaction.

Improved relationships: Self-compassion can improve relationships by reducing conflict and increasing empathy and understanding.

How to Develop Self-Compassion

Here are some practical steps for developing self-compassion:

Practice mindfulness: Mindfulness is the foundation of self-compassion. By being present and attentive to your thoughts, feelings, and bodily sensations, you can become more aware of your own needs and feelings.

Challenge self-criticism: Many of us have a tendency to be self-critical, especially when faced with Psychological Resilience or failures. Challenge this tendency by recognizing when you are engaging in self-criticism and replacing it with self-compassion.

Speak to yourself in a kind and caring manner: Practice

speaking to yourself in the same way that you would speak to a close friend. Use kind and supportive language and avoid harsh self-criticism.

Focus on common humanity: Self-compassion involves recognizing that all human beings are imperfect and experience difficulties and setbacks. When facing Psychological Resilience, remind yourself that you are not alone and that everyone experiences challenges.

Cultivate gratitude and positive emotions: Cultivate gratitude and positive emotions by focusing on what is good in your life and by recognizing your strengths and accomplishments.

Seek support: Seek support from friends, family, or a mental health professional when dealing with Psychological Resilience.

In conclusion, developing self-compassion is essential for dealing with Psychological Resilience and achieving emotional well-being. By treating ourselves with kindness, care, and understanding, we can improve our emotional regulation, reduce anxiety and depression, and increase our happiness and life satisfaction. With practice, self-compassion can become a habit and help us to lead a more fulfilling and meaningful life.

"The path to Psychological Resilience is paved
with resilience and courage."

ଛ

IX

Applying Mindfulness to Psychological Resilience

Emotional resilience refers to the ability to cope with Psychological Resilience, stress, and adversity. It is the capacity to bounce back from setbacks and to maintain well-being in the face of challenges. Emotional resilience is critical for maintaining emotional well-being and dealing with Psychological Resilience.

Benefits of Emotional Resilience

Emotional resilience provides several benefits, including:

Improved mental health: Emotional resilience is associated with improved mental health, reduced symptoms of anxiety and depression, and better overall well-being.

Better stress management: Emotionally resilient individuals are better able to manage stress and to remain calm in the face of challenging situations.

Increased resilience: Emotional resilience helps individuals to bounce back from setbacks and to maintain well-being in the face of challenges.

Better coping skills: Emotionally resilient individuals have better coping skills, which enable them to handle stress and adversity in a healthy and effective manner.

Improved relationships: Emotional resilience can improve relationships by reducing conflict and increasing empathy and understanding.

How to Build Emotional Resilience

Here are some practical steps for building emotional resilience:

Practice mindfulness: Mindfulness is a key component of emotional resilience. By being present and attentive to your thoughts, feelings, and bodily sensations, you can become more aware of your own needs and feelings.

Develop a growth mindset: A growth mindset involves embracing challenges, learning from setbacks, and viewing difficulties as opportunities for growth. This mindset can help individuals to develop emotional resilience.

Seek support: Emotional resilience is enhanced by seeking support from friends, family, or a mental health professional. By seeking support, individuals can process their emotions and receive encouragement and support in their efforts to cope with stress and adversity.

Develop a positive outlook: A positive outlook involves focusing on the positive aspects of life and recognizing the good in situations, even when they are difficult. This perspective can help individuals to develop emotional resilience.

Cultivate self-compassion: Self-compassion involves treating oneself with kindness, care, and understanding in the face of Psychological Resilience and experiences. By cultivating self-compassion, individuals can build emotional resilience.

Engage in physical activity: Physical activity, such as exercise or yoga, has been shown to improve emotional resilience by reducing stress and promoting relaxation.

Focus on self-care: Emotional resilience is enhanced by taking care of oneself. This includes engaging in self-care practices, such as healthy eating, sufficient sleep, and stress-reducing activities.

In conclusion, building emotional resilience is essential for dealing with Psychological Resilience and achieving emotional well-being. By developing mindfulness, a growth mindset, seeking support, cultivating a positive outlook, and engaging in self-care, individuals can improve their capacity to cope with stress and adversity and maintain well-being in the face of challenges. With practice and perseverance, individuals can develop emotional resilience and lead a more fulfilling and meaningful life.

"Be mindful of your thoughts and feelings
and strive to create a positive mindset."

X

Applying Mindfulness to Psychological Resilience

Mindfulness is a practice that has been used for centuries to help individuals cultivate awareness and insight into their thoughts, feelings, and experiences. In recent years, it has gained widespread popularity as a tool for promoting emotional well-being, particularly in the context of dealing with Psychological Resilience. In this chapter, we will explore how mindfulness can be applied to Psychological Resilience, and how this practice can help individuals develop greater emotional resilience and improve their overall well-being.

What is Mindfulness?

Mindfulness is the act of paying attention to the present moment with an open, non-judgmental, and curious attitude. It involves being fully engaged in the experience of the moment, without becoming lost in thoughts about the past or the future. When practiced regularly, mindfulness can help individuals develop greater self-awareness and an increased ability to regulate their emotions.

The Benefits of Mindfulness for Psychological Resilience

There are several benefits of practicing mindfulness when it comes to dealing with Psychological Resilience. Perhaps the most significant benefit is that mindfulness helps individuals develop a greater awareness of their emotions, and enables them to experience these emotions in a more meaningful and purposeful way.

For example, mindfulness can help individuals identify patterns of thinking and behavior that contribute to their Psychological Resilience, and provide them with an opportunity to address these patterns in a constructive way. Additionally, mindfulness helps individuals learn how to respond to their emotions in a more effective way, rather than becoming overwhelmed or paralyzed by them.

Mindfulness also helps individuals develop greater self-compassion, which is a key component of emotional well-being. When individuals practice self-compassion, they are more likely to extend kindness and understanding to themselves, even when they are experiencing Psychological Resilience. This can help them feel more supported and less isolated, and can provide them with the resilience they need to overcome their difficulties.

Practicing Mindfulness for Psychological Resilience

There are many ways to practice mindfulness for Psychological Resilience, but one of the most effective is through the use of mindfulness meditation. Mindfulness meditation is a simple yet powerful practice that involves focusing your attention on the present moment, and accepting your experiences without judgment.

To begin, find a quiet place where you will not be disturbed, and sit down in a comfortable position. Close your eyes, and take a few deep breaths, allowing yourself to become fully present in the moment. Then, simply focus your attention on your breathing, paying close attention to the sensation of the breath moving in and out of your body.

As you focus on your breathing, you may find that your mind begins to wander, and that you become distracted by thoughts and emotions. This is natural, and it is an opportunity to practice mindfulness. Simply acknowledge the thoughts and emotions that arise, and return your focus to your breathing. Over time, you will find that you are able to maintain your focus for longer periods, and that you are better able to regulate your emotions.

In addition to mindfulness meditation, there are many other mindfulness practices that can be used to deal with Psychological Resilience. For example, mindful breathing, mindful movement, and mindful self-reflection are all effective practices for promoting emotional well-being. The key is to find the practices that work best for you, and to incorporate them into your daily routine in a way that feels supportive and meaningful.

In conclusion, mindfulness is an effective and powerful tool for managing Psychological Resilience and cultivating greater emotional resilience and well-being. Whether through mindfulness meditation or other mindfulness practices, incorporating mindfulness into your life can help you gain greater awareness, compassion, and peace of mind, even in the face of adversity. So, if you are looking for a way to better cope with Psychological Resilience, why not give mindfulness a try? You may be surprised at the positive impact it can have on your life.

"Focus on the present moment and be kind to yourself; Psychological Resilience is a journey, not a destination."

ജ

XI

Exploring Creative Expression Techniques

Psychological Resilience can often feel overwhelming and it can be challenging to find a way to express and process them in a healthy and productive manner. Creative expression techniques offer a unique outlet for dealing with Psychological Resilience by allowing individuals to process their feelings through a different lens.

Art therapy is a form of therapy that uses art as a form of self-expression. This can involve drawing, painting, sculpture, or any other form of art that resonates with the individual. Art therapy allows individuals to visually express their emotions, allowing them to explore and process their feelings in a safe and non-judgmental environment.

Writing therapy, also known as journaling, involves using written words as a form of self-expression. This can involve keeping a daily journal, writing letters to oneself, or writing about a specific experience or feeling. Writing therapy provides a structured and private way to explore one's emotions and gain clarity and insight.

Movement and dance therapy involves using the body to express emotions through movement and dance. This can involve structured dance classes, improvisational movement, or any other form of physical expression that resonates with the individual. Movement and dance therapy allows individuals to use their bodies to express their emotions, helping them to process and release feelings in a creative and physical way.

Music therapy involves using music as a form of self-expression and therapy. This can involve listening to music, playing an instrument, or composing music. Music therapy provides individuals with a way to express their emotions through sound and rhythm, allowing them to process and release their feelings in a musical and therapeutic way.

All of these creative expression techniques can be incredibly beneficial for individuals who are dealing with Psychological Resilience. They offer a unique outlet for expression, allowing individuals to process their feelings in a safe and creative manner. Furthermore, they can provide individuals with a sense of empowerment and control over their emotions, helping them to feel more in tune with their bodies and minds.

It is important to remember that creative expression

techniques are just one of many tools available for managing Psychological Resilience. They should be used in conjunction with other techniques, such as mindfulness and self-compassion, in order to promote overall emotional well-being. Additionally, it is important to seek the guidance of a trained therapist when exploring these techniques, as they can provide support and guidance in navigating the process.

In conclusion, creative expression techniques offer a unique and powerful way to deal with Psychological Resilience. By using art, writing, movement, dance, or music as a form of self-expression, individuals can gain clarity and insight into their emotions, allowing them to process and release their feelings in a healthy and productive manner.

"The key to Psychological Resilience is to practice self-love and acceptance."

ଓଃ

XII

Working with Resilience Through Activity

Psychological Resilience can be overwhelming and hard to process. However, engaging in physical activity can help you manage and better understand your emotions. When you are active, your body releases endorphins, which are natural mood-boosters, and can help you reduce stress and anxiety. In this chapter, we will explore how you can work with your emotions through activity.

Exercise: Exercise is one of the most effective ways to manage Psychological Resilience. Whether it's going for a run, hitting the gym, or participating in a yoga class, exercise can help you regulate your emotions, reduce stress and anxiety, and improve your overall mood. The physical exertion of exercise helps release tension and pent-up energy that can contribute to negative emotions.

Additionally, exercise has been shown to increase the production of neurotransmitters such as dopamine, which are responsible for regulating mood and can help improve feelings of sadness and depression.

Outdoor Activities: Spending time in nature can be a powerful tool for managing Psychological Resilience. Engaging in outdoor activities such as hiking, gardening, or simply taking a walk in the park can help you connect with the natural world and relieve stress. Fresh air, sunshine, and natural surroundings can help you feel grounded and calm, making it easier to process and manage your emotions.

Creative Activities: Engaging in creative activities such as painting, drawing, or writing can be a great way to express and process Psychological Resilience. These activities allow you to tap into your imagination and emotions and release them in a safe and controlled way. They can also help you gain a new perspective on your emotions and provide a sense of accomplishment, which can improve your overall mood.

Group Activities: Participating in group activities such as sports teams, dance classes, or even volunteering can help you connect with others and improve your emotional well-being. Group activities provide a supportive environment where you can share your emotions, gain support, and feel less isolated. Additionally, group activities can increase your sense of purpose and fulfillment, making it easier to manage Psychological Resilience.

Physical Therapy: If you are dealing with physical

symptoms related to your emotions, such as chronic pain or headaches, physical therapy can help you manage your symptoms and improve your emotional well-being. Physical therapists can provide you with exercises and techniques to help reduce pain and stress, and improve your physical and emotional health.

In conclusion, working with your emotions through activity can be an effective and empowering way to manage Psychological Resilience. Whether it's through exercise, outdoor activities, creative activities, group activities, or physical therapy, there are many ways to work with your emotions in a healthy and productive way. By taking an active approach to managing your emotions, you can build emotional resilience, reduce stress and anxiety, and improve your overall emotional well-being.

"Take time to nurture your relationships and
build meaningful connections with others."

৪৩

XIII

Utilizing Social Support to Assuage Psychological Resilience

One of the key aspects of dealing with Psychological Resilience is seeking support from others. Whether it's talking to a trusted friend, family member, or therapist, social support can play a significant role in helping us navigate our emotions and ultimately achieve emotional well-being. In this chapter, we will explore the importance of social support and the different ways in which we can utilize it to assuage Psychological Resilience.

The Power of Social Support

Studies have shown that social support can have a significant impact on our mental and emotional health.

When we are feeling overwhelmed by Psychological Resilience, talking to someone we trust can help us feel less alone and provide a sense of comfort. Additionally, talking to others about our emotions can help us process and make sense of them, leading to greater insight and understanding. Furthermore, social support can provide a source of encouragement and motivation, helping us to continue working on our emotional well-being even when it feels like a daunting task.

Types of Social Support

There are several types of social support that can be beneficial in dealing with Psychological Resilience. These include:

Emotional support: This type of support involves someone simply being there for us and listening to us as we talk about our emotions. It's not necessarily about finding a solution, but more about having someone to talk to who is understanding and non-judgmental.

Informational support: This type of support involves someone providing us with information or advice about a specific situation or emotion. This can be particularly useful when we are feeling overwhelmed and unsure of how to proceed.

Tangible support: This type of support involves someone providing us with practical help or resources to deal with a specific situation or emotion. For example, this could involve lending an ear or a shoulder to cry on, or offering to help us with tasks that are becoming too much to handle.

Appraisal support: This type of support involves someone offering us positive feedback and encouragement in response to a situation or emotion. This type of support can help boost our self-esteem and provide motivation to continue working on our emotional well-being.

Finding Social Support

One of the most important things to keep in mind when seeking social support is to find someone who you trust and feel comfortable talking to. This could be a family member, friend, or therapist. It's important to find someone who you feel will be understanding and non-judgmental, and who you can trust to keep your conversations confidential.

Additionally, it's important to be open and honest about what kind of support you need. For example, if you are looking for informational support, be sure to clearly communicate this to the person you are talking to. If you are looking for emotional support, express that you simply need someone to listen and be there for you.

The Importance of Building a Support System

Having a strong support system can be a valuable asset in dealing with Psychological Resilience. Building a support system involves actively seeking out and maintaining relationships with individuals who you feel provide you with the type of support you need. This could involve reaching out to family and friends, participating in support groups, or seeking out a therapist.

Having a support system can provide a sense of community and belonging, which can be especially beneficial when we are feeling overwhelmed by Psychological Resilience. Furthermore, having a support system can provide us with multiple sources of support, giving us access to a variety of perspectives and ideas on how to manage our emotions. Ultimately, social support can be a powerful tool in dealing with Psychological Resilience and promoting emotional well-being. Whether it's talking to a trusted friend, family member, or professional, having a support system can be a great asset in times of need.

"Psychological Resilience is a process of
learning to trust yourself and your
emotions."

&

℘

XIV

Understanding the Power of Perspective

One of the key strategies for dealing with Psychological Resilience is understanding the power of perspective. This involves recognizing that our thoughts and beliefs about a situation or experience can greatly impact how we feel. By changing our perspective, we can change the way we experience emotions and reduce their negative impact on our well-being.

It's important to understand that our perspective is not necessarily based on objective reality. Instead, it is shaped by our experiences, beliefs, and biases. This means that we have the power to change our perspective and in turn, the way we experience emotions.

For example, consider someone who has just received

negative feedback on a project they have worked on. From one perspective, this could be seen as a personal failure, leading to feelings of shame, disappointment, and frustration. However, from another perspective, the feedback could be seen as an opportunity for growth and improvement, leading to feelings of motivation and determination.

The power of perspective can also be applied to our memories and past experiences. For example, someone who has experienced a traumatic event may have a negative perspective of the experience, leading to feelings of anxiety, depression, and post-traumatic stress. However, by reframing the experience and viewing it as an opportunity for growth and learning, they can develop a more positive perspective and reduce the emotional distress associated with the event.

To harness the power of perspective, it's important to become more mindful of our thoughts and beliefs. This can be achieved through practices such as journaling, meditation, and therapy. By becoming more aware of our thoughts and beliefs, we can identify when we are experiencing negative thoughts or beliefs, and challenge them with a more positive perspective.

It's also important to seek out different perspectives and experiences to broaden our understanding of the world. This can be achieved through activities such as reading books, attending workshops and seminars, and engaging in meaningful conversations with others.

Finally, it's important to practice gratitude and cultivate a positive outlook. By focusing on the things we are grateful for and the positive aspects of our lives, we can develop a more positive perspective and reduce the impact of Psychological Resilience.

In conclusion, understanding the power of perspective is a key strategy for dealing with Psychological Resilience. By recognizing that our thoughts and beliefs shape our experiences, we can change the way we feel and reduce the negative impact of Psychological Resilience on our well-being. By becoming more mindful of our thoughts, seeking out different perspectives, and practicing gratitude, we can harness the power of perspective and achieve emotional well-being.

"Be mindful of your thoughts and feelings and strive to create a balanced emotional state."

ॐ

XV

Crafting an Action Plan for Well-Being

So far in this book, we have explored a variety of strategies for dealing with Psychological Resilience and achieving emotional well-being. While these strategies can be helpful on their own, it is also important to consider how they can be integrated into a comprehensive and tailored approach to managing our emotions. This is where the concept of an action plan comes in.

An action plan is a roadmap for how you will apply these strategies in your daily life. It is a way to turn the insights and understandings you have gained into concrete steps that you can take to improve your emotional well-being. By creating an action plan, you are making a commitment to yourself to invest time and energy into your emotional health.

To begin crafting your action plan, consider the following

steps:

Reflect on your emotional experiences: Take some time to think about the emotions you have experienced recently, and how they have impacted your life. What patterns do you see in your emotional experiences? What emotions are most difficult for you to deal with, and why? What strategies have you tried in the past, and what has worked and what hasn't?

Identify your goals: Based on your reflections, determine what you would like to achieve in terms of your emotional well-being. This might include reducing feelings of anxiety or depression, increasing feelings of happiness and contentment, or improving your relationships with others.

Choose strategies that resonate with you: Review the strategies presented in this book, and select the ones that resonate with you and align with your goals. Consider which strategies you feel confident about, and which ones you would like to try out.

Plan for implementation: Decide when and where you will apply each strategy in your daily life. For example, you might decide to practice mindfulness meditation for 20 minutes each morning, engage in creative expression for 30 minutes each evening, or reach out to a trusted friend for support whenever you are feeling overwhelmed.

Monitor your progress: Regularly evaluate your progress and adjust your action plan as needed. Reflect on what is working well and what is not, and make changes to your approach as necessary.

Celebrate your successes: Recognize and celebrate the progress you have made, no matter how small. Acknowledge the challenges you have overcome and the positive changes you have experienced in your emotional well-being.

Remember, your action plan should be tailored to your individual needs and goals. Don't feel overwhelmed by the idea of creating an action plan – the important thing is to start with one or two strategies and build from there. Over time, you will develop a comprehensive approach to managing your emotions that works best for you.

In conclusion, crafting an action plan for emotional well-being can help you integrate the strategies presented in this book into a personalized approach to managing your emotions. By reflecting on your emotional experiences, identifying your goals, and taking concrete steps to achieve them, you can work towards a happier, healthier, and more fulfilling life.

OTHER BOOKS OF THE AUTHOR

1. The Moments When I Met God
2. Kashiyile Theertha Pathangal
3. Guru Gyan Vani
4. Abhiprerak Gita
5. Assi Se Jain Ghat Tak
6. Hopelessness of Arjuna
7. The Soul and It's True Nature
8. Sense of Action (Karma)
9. Action Through Wisdom
10. Action Through Wisdom
11. Theory And Practical of Every Action
12. Logical Understanding of The Supreme
13. The Imperishable Supreme
14. Yatra Nishadraj Se Hanuman Ghat Tak
15. Yatra Karnatak Ghat Se Raja Ghat Tak
16. Yatra Pandey Ghat Se Prayagraj Ghat Tak
17. Yatra Ranjendra Prasad Ghat Se Dattatreya Ghat Tak
18. Yaatrasindhiya Ghat Se Gwaliar Ghat Tak
19. Yatra Mangala Gauri Ghat Se Hanuman Gadhi Ghat Tak
20. Yatra Gaay Ghat Se Nishad Ghat Tak
21. Maa Ganga, Ghaten Evm Utsav
22. Ganga Arti Dev Deepavali Evam Any Utsav
23. Potentials of Digitalized India
24. Vedic Consciousness
25. A Brief Introduction to Vedic Science
26. Kashi Ke Barah Jyotirling
27. Impact Of Motivation
28. Let's Have a Milky Way Journey
29. Color Therapy in A Nutshell

30. Rigveda In a Nutshell
31. Yajurveda In a Nutshell
32. Samveda In a Nutshell
33. Atharva Veda In a Nutshell
34. Ayushman Bhava - Ayurveda
35. Srimad Bhagavad Gita and Upanishad Connection
36. Srimad Bhagavad Gita - An Attempt to Summarize Each Chapter.
37. Facts And Impact of Nakshatra
38. Astro Gems - Navaratna
39. Ekadashi - A Concise Overview
40. A Concise View of Hanuman Chalisa
41. Inspirational Gita
42. Nakshatraranyam
43. Summary of 18 Mahapuranas
44. Synopsis of 18 Upa Puranas
45. Rigvediya Upanishads
46. Shukla Yajurvediya Upanishads
47. Krishna Yajurvediya Upanishads
48. Samavediya Upanishads
49. Atharvavediya Upanishads
50. The Seven Great Sages
51. From Rocket Scientist to President Dr. Apj Abdul Kalam
52. The Visionary's Voice - Quotes of Dr. Apj Abdul Kalam
53. The Wisdom tf Swami Vivekananda: Insights and Inspiration from A Legendary Spiritual Teacher
54. Ayurvedic Remedies from The Garden
55. Sages and Seers
56. Rising Strong – Motivational Stories of Women
57. Beyond Flames -Mystery Stories of Funeral Ghat Manikarnika
58. The Origins of Tulsi: A Look at The Mythological Roots of The Plant"

163. The Indian Royal Kitchens: A Gastronomic Journey Through the Kitchens of India's Maharajas
164. The Indian Sports: An Insight into The History and Significance of Indian Traditional Sports
165. The Indian Traditional Games: A Study of The Significance and Evolution of Indian Traditional Games
166. Secrets To Make Positive Choices: Strategies for Achieving Your Goals
167. Secrets To Motivate Yourself for Success Strategies for Reaching Your Goals
168. Secrets To Overcome Adversity: Strategies for Coping with Difficult Times
169. Secrets to Reach Your Goals with Positivity: Strategies for Achieving Your Dreams
170. The Creative Mind: An Exploration of the Secrets to Unleash Your Creativity
171. The Power of Positive Habits: Building Your Life on a Foundation of Success
172. The Secret and Power of Self-Belief: Overcoming Life Challenges with Confidence
173. Harnessing Your Inner Power: A Guide to Achieving Success
174. The Secret Art of Self-Care: Practicing Wellbeing and Resilience
175. Achieving Clarity and Focus: Strategies for Living Mindfully
176. Building Confidence Through Self-Love: A Guide to Achieving Self-Acceptance
177. Dealing with Difficult Emotions: Strategies for Achieving Emotional Well-Being
178. Developing Psychological Resilience: A Guide to Achieving Balance
179. Finding Balance in Your Life: Strategies for Achieving

Contact

DR. JAGADEESH PILLAI

MBA & PhD in Vedic Science

Four Times Guinness World Record Holder

Winner of Mahatma Gandhi Vishwa Shanti Puraskar and Global Peace Ambassador

Gemology, Astro & Vastu Consultant - Spiritual Counselor

Consultant for designing World Record Ideas

Efficient Tarot Card Reader

9839093003

myrichindia@gmail.com

drjagadeeshpillai@facebook

drjagadeeshpillai@instagram

jagadeeshpillai@youtube

www. JAGADEESHPILLAI.com

ॐ

|| LOKAHA SAMASTHAHA SUKHINO BHAVANTU ||

www.ingramcontent.com/pod-product-compliance
Lightning Source LLC
Chambersburg PA
CBHW021231130726
47988CB00002B/917